Controlling Anger

....

Responding Constructively
When Life Goes Wrong

David Powlison

New
Growth
Press

newgrowthpress.com

New Growth Press, Greensboro, NC 27401
newgrowthpress.com
Copyright © 2008 by Christian Counseling & Educational
Foundation.

Cover Design: The DesignWorks Group, Nate Salciccioli and
Jeff Miller, www.thedesignworksgroup.com

Typesetting: Robin Black, www.blackbirdcreative.biz

ISBN: 978-1-939946-60-7 (Print)
ISBN: 978-1-934885-42-0 (eBook)

Printed in India
29 28 27 26 25 24 23   8 9 10 11

What makes you angry? Sometimes small things make us angry: traffic jams, lines at the grocery store, not being able to find a shoe, a waiter's mistake, or a friend's inattention. And sometimes big things make us angry: betrayal, injustice, meanness, violence, oppression, selfishness, and lying. When we see and experience such things firsthand, we get angry.

How do you deal with your anger? Do you explode? Does everyone around you know when and why you are angry? Or are you more subtle? Do you get irritated and short with those around you? Do you gossip and complain about your spouse, children, coworkers, and friends? Or maybe you just turn your anger in on yourself and become depressed and bitter.

You might have noticed that you can't avoid dealing with your anger. Anger is an inevitable response to living in a troubled world where things can and do go wrong all the time. God does care about what makes you angry, but he also cares about how you express anger. If you don't learn how to deal with your anger, you will become bitter and estranged from God and people.

Venting? Calming? Or God's Way?

Some counselors notice that people get tied up in knots when they stuff their anger. They will tell you to deal with your anger by getting in touch with how you feel and then expressing it. "Get it off your chest. Say exactly what you think. Give 'em a piece of your mind."

Other counselors notice how destructive people become when they express anger. They will counsel you to control your anger. Psychotherapy, medication, exercise, and meditation are just some of the different ways they recommend for defusing your anger and calming yourself down.

So which is it, venting or calming? God has a different way for you to deal with your anger. God knows well that stuffing your anger deep inside is destructive. And learning tricks for keeping calm never discovers the purpose for which God designed anger. Anger needs to be acknowledged and expressed in a positive way, as a form of doing what is good and right.

At the same time, God knows that venting your anger is destructive. Anger needs to be expressed constructively. Instead of expressing your anger destructively, God's way is for you to express your anger in a way that actually redeems difficult situations and relationships. How does this happen? It starts with understanding what anger is, where it comes from, and how a right relationship with God will actually change the way you view and express your anger.

What Is Anger?

Anger always expresses two things: It identifies something in your world that *matters* to you, and it proclaims that you believe that something is *wrong*. This could be something as minor as being served a cold cup of coffee at a restaurant. It could be something as major as your spouse running off with your best friend. Anger is our God-given capacity to respond to a wrong that we think is important. God also gets angry at things that are wrong in this world. Your capacity to be angry is an expression of being made in his image. So when you get angry, you are not necessarily wrong. But often our anger does go wrong. What are some ways that anger goes wrong?

Ways That Anger Goes Wrong

Anger goes wrong when we get angry about things that don't matter. God's anger is always holy and pure because what he says is wrong *is* wrong, and what he says matters *does* matter. God is rightly displeased when people are harmed and hurt by others. "Love does no harm to its neighbor" (Romans 13:10). God says, "Never pay back evil for evil" (Romans 12:17, NASB). Two wrongs never make a right, and our anger often simply doubles the wrong. But God's anger makes right what is wrong (Romans 12:19).

One difference between our anger and God's anger is that, since we aren't always holy and pure, we often get angry at things that aren't true wrongs and don't really matter to anyone but us. If you throw a tantrum when you are served cold food in a restaurant, or curse when you are stuck in traffic, or _____ (fill in the blank with those things that push your buttons)—these are not things that really matter in God's world.

God explains to us in the Bible why we get angry at things that don't really matter to anyone but us. The apostle Paul uses the phrase "the desire of the flesh" (Galatians 5:16–17, NASB) to describe where our wrong anger comes from. You and I get angry because of what we desire (what we expect, want, and believe we need) to happen in a certain situation or relationship.

Think about the last time you got angry. Underneath your angry feelings, words, and actions is what you wanted but didn't get. Respect, affirmation, power, convenience, cooperation, help, money, comfort, intimacy, peace, pleasure, identity, safety...what is it that you want? And how do you respond when you don't get it? Anger going wrong loudly tells the world, "I want my way! My will be done!"

Anger goes wrong when we want a good thing more than we want God. Sometimes we want good things.

It's not wrong to want your husband to love and listen to you. It's not wrong to want your children to respect and obey you. It's not wrong to want your boss to be honest with you. It's not wrong to want a warm meal and a hot cup of coffee, or to get to your appointment rather than getting stuck in traffic. But when fulfilling your desires, even for a good thing, becomes more important than anything else, that's when it changes into a "desire of the flesh." You want it too much. When you don't get what you want, demand, believe you need, and think you deserve, your anger flares up.

James, in the letter he wrote to the early church, said this about where our wrong anger comes from: "What causes fights and quarrels among you? Don't they come from your desires that battle within you? You want something but don't get it. You kill and covet, but you cannot have what you want. You quarrel and fight..." (James 4:1–2). When you want anything—even a good thing—more than God, you will get angry when you don't get it or it's taken away from you.

Anger goes wrong when you respond to a true wrong in the wrong way. Sometimes we are right to be angry, because we are experiencing a true wrong. Then the problem is not getting angry, but how we express our anger. It's not right for someone to tailgate you, recklessly and aggressively endangering you and your family. It's not right when your spouse is indifferent or inconsiderate. It's not right if your boss treats you unfairly or your child refuses to obey. It's not right when you are abused or attacked.

Anger has been given to us by God as the way to say, "That's not right and that matters." In our broken world, you will have many good reasons to be angry. But because we are part of the broken world, we express our anger at true wrongs in the wrong way. We blow up. We get irritated. We gossip. We complain. We hold a grudge. We shut people out. We get even. We become embittered, cynical, hostile. Something really wrong happened…and we become really wrong in reaction.

How can we learn to sort all this out? How can we change?

Change Starts with Your Relationship with God

What's behind all of your wrong anger? When you get angry aren't you taking God's place and judging others, even judging God? Whether you are angry about something trivial or something serious, your wrong reaction reveals that you are living as if *you* are in charge of the world. You believe *you* have the right to judge the people around you and the way God is running the world.

When James talks about anger, he goes on to discuss why it's wrong to judge and criticize others: "There is only one Lawgiver and Judge, the one who is able to save and destroy. But you—who are you to judge your neighbor?" (James 4:12). God alone has the right to pass final judgment. Think about when you get angry. Aren't you insisting, "My will be done; my kingdom come"? And when things don't go your way, don't you judge those (including God) who are not doing what you want, as if you were God? You aren't God, but when you are angry, you often act as if you were.

Because your wrong anger has to do with your relationship with God, you can't deal with it by learning a few strategies or techniques. Wrong anger creates a big problem between you and God. He doesn't like upstarts who try to take over his universe. Your anger is not just about you and all the frustrating things that happen to you. It's not just about you and your cranky, oppositional personality. And it's not just about you and all the unreasonable people in your life. It's about you, those frustrating circumstances, all those unreasonable people…and the living God. It's about you acting like you are in charge of God's world and other people. But God is in charge.

Acting as if you are God—pride—is the beating heart of what it means to be a sinner. This insight into anger is hugely freeing and very sobering. Anger going wrong testifies to our pride. When you see yourself as a sinner, instead of focusing on how everyone around you is wrong, then God's grace and mercy is available to you. God's mercy is for those who honestly confess their sins to him and ask for the grace to change. James also says, "God opposes the proud but gives grace to the humble" (James 4:6; see 4:7–10 for more details on what's involved in turning to God).

Anger is merciless. Anger sees, punishes, and gets rid of all offenders. But God has chosen to be merciful to wrongdoers, including someone like you, who struggles with taking God's place in the world (Ephesians 2:1–5). God's mercy brings life to you. If you struggle with bitterness, if you grumble, if you yell and argue, then you need God's mercy. You will receive mercy and help when you confess to God your struggle with trying to control everything, with wanting to be God, and with judging those around you. God's just anger toward sinners like you was poured out on his Son on the cross. Because Jesus died, you can be forgiven and have a whole new life.

When you honestly confess your sins to God and ask him to forgive you for Jesus' sake, you will receive forgiveness and the gift of God's Spirit. The Spirit will give you the power to express your anger not your way, but God's way.

God's Anger Is Redemptive; Yours Can Be Too

How does God respond when something important in his world is wrong? He responds redemptively. Is God angry when people act like their own god, playing false to him, and bringing grief to themselves and others? Yes. But how did he express that anger? By sending his very own Son to this broken world to be broken on the cross. He sacrificed his Son so his people can be forgiven, transformed, and restored to a right relationship with him and others.

Your anger can also result in redemption. When you come to God and find forgiveness for Jesus' sake, you will be filled with God's Spirit. Because you are filled with his Spirit, it will be possible for you also to respond redemptively when you are angry. You can learn to say, "That's wrong," without ranting, exaggerating, cursing, yelling, or name calling.

What Matters to God Will Matter to You

Being filled with the Spirit means everything about you will start to resemble God. Instead of responding with sinful anger to unimportant things, you will start to see your life from God's perspective. You will begin to care about things that truly matter, instead of overreacting to relatively unimportant things.

When Jesus was on earth, he was not a stoic. No one cared more than he did about the things that were wrong in this world. He cared so much that he gave his life to right those wrongs. But his upset was driven by faith and love, not by pettiness, hostility, and aggression. Becoming like God means that you will care about the things Jesus cares about—the things that truly matter in God's world.

React Constructively to a True Wrong

Becoming like God means that, when you see a true wrong, you will learn to respond the way God does. When God sees a true wrong he responds constructively. He has done this toward us, by naming our wrongs clearly, and then offering us the mercy and grace we do not deserve. Here are some ways that God responds constructively to a true wrong:

- *God is patient.* Patience literally means slow to anger. God is described in the Bible as "slow to anger" (Exodus 34:6). Learning to be "slow to anger" means living in a world that has things wrong in it—an unloving spouse, an unfair boss, a disrespectful teenager—and being willing to stay in difficult situations and relationships for the long haul. Why? Because you realize that you live in God's world, not your own, and though this wrong needs to be addressed, your call from God is to persevere in addressing it constructively, patiently, and kindly.

• *God is merciful.* Mercy is a way of looking at something that is wrong and saying, "I'm going to tackle that to make it better." The mercy of God is a constructive displeasure. God could respond with wrath, but instead, he sets about making right what is wrong. Because God is merciful, he sent Jesus to die on the cross for you. His just anger was poured out on Jesus. God's mercy means you are spared the consequences of your rebellion against him. As you experience God's mercy, you will learn to be merciful. Instead of angrily judging others, you will roll up your sleeves and help to right the wrongs you see.

• *God is forgiving.* God's forgiveness doesn't make what was wrong okay. He names what is wrong (including our wrongful anger!) and deals with the wrong by paying the price himself.

Forgiveness is a way to be displeased in a constructive way. Instead of insisting on justice right now, forgiveness acknowledges the wrong and lets it go. When you love your enemy by treating him or her kindly, you are overcoming evil with good. Loving someone who's done wrong is the way to overcome that wrong.

• *God confronts in love.* There is a place for a right kind of anger, an anger whose purpose is love. Because God lovingly confronts, so can you. For example, abusers and those who do evil to others should be brought to justice. It is both constructive and loving for wrongdoers to face the consequences of their wrongs. If your child is disrespectful, you should be upset, and there should be consequences. But what do you do with that upset? Do you rant and rave? Become physically abusive? No, your anger can be constructively expressed as a clear reprimand and fair consequences. You are forceful, but your forcefulness is motivated by love for your child.

The Opposite of Sinful Anger

The opposite of sinful anger is not ignoring what's truly wrong in this world. Instead, godly anger constructively engages what is wrong in a way that is patient, merciful, forgiving, and honest in tackling what needs tackling. Our sinful anger causes hurt, destruction, and alienation. Godly anger becomes an instrument in God's hands to make this bad world better.

Practical Strategies for Change

God's way of dealing with what is wrong in this world is wonderful and surprising, combining firmness with gentleness, honesty with forgiveness. But how do you put it into practice? How do you learn to let go of your wrong anger and express your just anger constructively? Paul gives you practical help in his letter to the Ephesians. He says this about how to handle your anger:

> Do not let any unwholesome talk come out of
> your mouths, but only what is helpful for building
> others up according to their needs, that it may
> benefit those who listen. And do not grieve the
> Holy Spirit of God, with whom you were sealed
> for the day of redemption. Get rid of all bitterness,
> rage and anger, brawling and slander, along with
> every form of malice. Be kind and compassionate
> to one another, forgiving each other, just as in
> Christ God forgave you. Be imitators of God,
> therefore, as dearly loved children and live a life of

love, just as Christ loved us and gave himself up
for us as a fragrant offering and sacrifice to God.
(Ephesians 4:29—5:2)

Paul starts by telling us how *not* to express our
anger. First, he says we are not to keep to ourselves and
brood ("bitterness"). Second, he says we are not to go to
the other person and dump our anger ("rage and anger").
Finally, we shouldn't go to others who aren't involved
and gossip ("slander"). So, if you can't stuff your anger,
or blow up, or gossip, what's left to do?!

Go to God

You have to go to God for help. As you go to him, you
will learn how to think through your angry reactions,
how to go to other people in such a way that you're
actually asking for help, and how to go to the other
person in a way that's constructive. Your anger will be
transformed when you understand deep in your heart
how God, in Christ, treats you. God's patience, mercy,
forgiveness, and loving confrontation will only become
real in your life as your relationship with him grows.
Start with an honest meeting with God.

Here are four questions to ask yourself, and then
one thing you need to do that will direct your honest
meeting with God.

1. *What is happening around me when I get angry?*
   What pushes your buttons? Think of specific times
   when you become angry. Make a list of the last five
   times you got angry, or keep track of the next five
   times. Describe what was going on around you.
   Now look back at the ways your anger went wrong.
   Sort out your list into the different ways that anger
   can go either wrong or right. When did you get
   angry at something that doesn't really matter in
   God's world? When did you get angry because you
   had made a good thing more important than God?
   And when did you get angry because you were
   truly wronged?

2. *How do I act when I get angry?* Look at your list
   and write down what you do when your anger goes
   wrong. Do you express your anger in bitterness
   (stuffing your anger)? In arguing (in expressing
   your anger freely to those around you)? In slander (gossiping and talking about those who have
   wronged you)? Or in some combination of all
   three? Be detailed in your description of how your
   wrongful anger gets expressed. Were there any
   times when anger actually was an expression of
   love, not hate, and was expressed constructively?

3. *What were my expectations (what did I want, need, demand) when I became angry?* This question about your motives brings God into the discussion, because it reveals what hijacked God's place in your heart. Your answer will show you where you need God's help the most. This will take your focus off of the circumstances that were the occasion for your anger and help you to think about why you believed you had a right to be angry *and* a right to express your anger in the way you did.

4. *What message does God, in his Word, have for me that will speak to my anger?* Think back to what James says is the cause of our anger. We get sinfully angry when we forget that God, not us, is in charge of the world. If you remember that this is God's kingdom and not yours, the way you deal with anger will be hugely affected. When you add to that an understanding of your real sins, then you will also see how God, in Christ, is tenderhearted and forgiving to you. Your anger will be transformed. Remembering the height, the depth, the width, and the length of God's love and mercy toward you will put your circumstances and your angry response in the right perspective (Ephesians 3:14–19). Meditating on your need for mercy and

God's forgiveness will remind you that no matter
what is making you angry, it's so much less than
what you have been given in Christ.

5. *Ask God for help.* You must turn to God for help
if your wrong anger patterns are going to change.
Turn to the God who loves you and tell him all
about what is making you angry. Name your suffering, your expectations, your desires, your sins,
and all the evil you see and do, and bring yourself
to the one who suffered and died for you.

In your honest conversation with God, use the Psalms.
God has given us the Psalms so we have many different
ways of talking with God about the things that really matter to us. Some psalms speak to God about our sins: e.g.,
Psalms 32 and 51. Other psalms speak about suffering
injustice at the hands of others: e.g., Psalms 10 and 31. And
many psalms speak of both: e.g., Psalms 25 and 119. All
the psalms speak of God and reveal what he is like, what
we need from him, and how we express love for him. The
Psalms are poetic, but they are not poetry; they are living
examples given to teach us how to talk honestly with God
about things that matter. Your relationship with a living
person is what sets the Bible's approach to anger apart from
self-help books, medications, and mind control. Being in

relationship with the living God is what will gradually change your anger from destructive to constructive.

What Am I Called to Do?

Your relationship with God will always lead you to your relationship with people. If you have gone through all these questions, then you don't need a prescription that says, "Do A, B, and C." Because you are in relationship with a living person, there will be a living quality to your wisdom. Perhaps at the moment you start to complain about the waitress and cold coffee, you will realize, *You know what? That was just so selfish. Lord have mercy upon me.* And then you might even turn to the people you're eating dinner with and say, "You know, my attitude really stunk just now and I'm sorry." And it's the right thing for you to apologize to the waitress too! Think of how that will make her day—a customer willing to treat her like a person, not just whine out of entitlement and self-righteousness. Then bring up the problem of the cold coffee in a reasonable way.

Everyone gets angry, but some people are more easily irritated than others. Can a cranky person learn to deal with anger God's way also? One of the wonderful things about God is that our characteristic struggles are not news to him. There are some people who are more feisty and irritable than others. Each of us has one or two areas where we are most likely to struggle. For some people it is in the area of anger. Others might struggle with fear, or comfort, or lust, or worries about money.

Your goal should not be to find *the* answer to your struggle, as if you could solve an anger problem once and for all. Instead, your struggle with anger will prove to be the door through which you learn to depend on God. Your irritability shows you how much you need God. Because of it you can see that you need his mercy, his forgiveness, and his help every day. Others who struggle with fear learn the same things as their fears bring them to their need to ask God for help.

All of our sins express how something potentially good has gone bad. We've mentioned how even anger can be something right and constructive. The good part in your struggle with wrongful anger is that you probably have been given a strong sense of justice and fairness. As you grow in wisdom and self-control, your desire for justice will be expressed not in irritation at the people around you, but in a willingness to work with them to right the wrongs you see. Perhaps without fully noticing it, you will become part of a constructive solution instead of a destructive force that makes things worse.

David Powlison

Jesus said, "Blessed are the peace*makers* [not the peace-lovers or peace-keepers who always avoid conflicts] because they will be called the sons of God" (Matthew 5:9). God uses his sense of justice and fairness to go to work at *making* peace with us, and then teaching us to make peace with each other. His children become like him.

No one can write the script for you on how to deal with your anger. But every time you notice that you are angry, go through those five questions. Then remind yourself of God's message of love and mercy to you. As you keep going to Jesus with everything in your heart, you will notice that, step by small step, real change is happening.

Your willingness to be mastered by Jesus and to make following him your first priority will allow you to imitate him in expressing your anger in a redemptive way. Then your conflicts won't end with slammed doors, hurt silences, and sharing others' sins. Instead, there will be a constructive back-and-forth that is colored by mercy and a desire for each of you to grow in God's image. Your real, living relationship with the God who loves you to the uttermost will allow you to grow in having real human relationships, where the conflicts you have will become an opportunity for growth, understanding, and expressing the fruits of the Spirit.

Simple, Quick, Biblical

Advice on Complicated Counseling Issues
for Pastors, Counselors, and Individuals

MINIBOOK
CATEGORIES

- Personal Change
- Marriage & Parenting
- Medical & Psychiatric Issues
- Women's Issues
- Singles
- Military